D0604023

CALGARY PUBLIC LIBRARY

VIKING STUDIO
Published by the Penguin Group, Penguin Putnam Inc.,
375 Hudson Street, New York, New York 10014, U.S.A.
Penguin Books Ltd, 27 Wrights Lane, London W8 5TZ, England
Penguin Books Australia Ltd, Ringwood, Victoria, Australia
Penguin Books Canada Ltd, 10 Alcorn Avenue,
Toronto, Ontario, Canada M4V 3B2
Penguin Books (N.Z.) Ltd, 182–190 Wairau Road,
Auckland 10, New Zealand

Penguin Books Ltd, Registered Offices:
Harmondsworth, Middlesex, England

First American edition published in 2000 by Viking Studio,
a member of Penguin Putnam Inc.

1 2 3 4 5 6 7 8 9 10

The Moon in the Pines copyright © Frances Lincoln Limited, 2000
Translations, introduction and notes copyright © Jonathan Clements, 2000
Afterword and captions by Bernd Jesse copyright © Frances Lincoln Limited, 2000

All rights reserved

Illustrations reproduced by permission of
The Art Institute of Chicago copyright © The Art Institute of Chicago

ISBN 0-670-89229-7

CIP data available

Tien Wah Press Pte Ltd, Singapore
Set in Baker Signet
Designed by Becky Clarke

Without limiting the rights under copyright reserved above, no part
of this publication may be reproduced, stored in or introduced into
a retrieval system, or transmitted, in any form or by any means (electronic,
mechanical, photocopying, recording or otherwise), without the prior written
permission of both the copyright owner and the above publisher of this book.

The Moon in the Pines

Zen Haiku

SELECTED AND TRANSLATED BY

JONATHAN CLEMENTS

ILLUSTRATED WITH JAPANESE PRINTS AND PAINTINGS
FROM THE ART INSTITUTE OF CHICAGO

VIKING STUDIO

For Kate Pankhurst - J. C.

CONTENTS

Introduction

Zen Buddhism is less a religion than a philosophy of living; a means of realizing the true nature of existence. It stresses the importance of fully embracing each moment of life; of reaching union with everything that is by penetrating as deeply as possible into the here and now. Zen therefore has a strong affinity with haiku, Japanese verse that is traditionally composed of seventeen syllables in three lines – the shortest form of poetry in the world. Haiku seeks, in a handful of words, to crystallize an instant in all its fullness, encouraging through the experience of the moment the union of the reader with all existence. The reader side-steps conventional perception, startled into a momentary but full understanding of the poet's experience. By locking reader and poet into the same reality, haiku helps us perceive the ultimate unity of all realities. Haiku transforms the most mundane of moments into something special. In Zen it is glimpses like these, rather than the study of doctrine, that are said to lead to enlightenment – the realization of the true nature of existence.

How can a good haiku so fully recreate the poet's experience in just a few words? As Zen, more than any other form of Buddhism, is a personal experience; so haiku, more than any other form of verse, requires the personal involvement of the reader. The haiku poet, knowing that words are not enough to capture the fullness of any moment, inscribes a partial idea that leaves an all-important space for the reader to fill in. As you question what the poet has omitted, the poem comes alive through your own memories and feelings. When Otsuji writes:

> Its sail dips in the sea
> The ship on the spring waters.

He does not need to say that the waters are rough, because we have seen the rocking of the sail on the waves. Nor does he need to say that we are watching from a safe position on the shore, since we have noticed the distant sail rather than the movement of the boat itself or the creaking of timbers. The poem tells us as much with omission as it does with inclusion.

Each haiku has its *kigo*, a word that, by referring to a particular season (and its natural colours and features), triggers a series of personal associations in the mind of the reader. Not all haiku need mention the season itself as Otsuji does here; sometimes the same effect is achieved through less direct means. There are many *kigo* – a few of the better-known include cherry blossoms, nightingales or willows (for spring); a welcoming evening breeze, dragonflies or lilies (for summer); the harvest moon, reddening leaves or scarecrows (for autumn); and mandarin ducks, frost or hail (for winter). By using *kigo* and individual associations, the reader spins a whole world of new ideas from a tiny string of words.

Although there have been poems similar to haiku for a very long time, it was only in the seventeenth century that the most famous of the haiku poets, Matsuo Bashō, formally established the seventeen-syllable, three-line structure of the haiku. He also set precedents for subject matter by writing verses on unexpected topics and seeking to bring a sense of poetical refinement to the most commonplace of occurrences. In Bashō's hands, the act of having an early meal in the garden becomes a many-layered poem:

> I break my fast
> Amidst the morning glory.

The haiku not only moves the reader's eye away from the simple meal to a pretty view but also reminds us to seize the day. As in English, morning glory has a double meaning since these flowers only bloom for a few hours. Bashō wrote the poem for a pupil whom he feared was ruining his health through overindulgence.

This collection presents nearly one hundred masterpieces of haiku, from the seminal seventeenth-century work of Bashō to poems from the early days of the twentieth. These new translations cast a fresh light on the poems, many of which are well-known. Most of the poems do not fit the traditional format of seventeen syllables in three lines – I have emphasized meaning and allusion over formal constraints in order to capture something of the Zen spirit of the originals. Haiku is usually organized chronologically, by poets' dates of birth, or seasonally, by the time of year they invoke. This book breaks with these traditions, grouping the poems instead by spiritual mood into four sections linked to times of the day. The anticipation of dawn, the bright energy of daylight, the melancholy of dusk and the silent reflection of moonlight – in Zen, as with so much in life, there can be four seasons in one day.

The poems are accompanied by Japanese prints and paintings that use techniques of empty space and symmetry to accomplish with pictures what haiku manage with words – each creating a beginning which viewers must complete with their own minds. At the back of the book is a selection of notes to the poems. I advise the reader to dip into the book at will, and to turn to the notes only when the book's supply of verse seems exhausted. The notes set the poems in their historical and personal context, adding another level of meaning that may well transform them once more. On a second reading, the poems will not be the same poems – and you will not be the same reader.

DAWN

In field nor mountain, nothing stirs

On this snowy morning.

CHIYO-NI

But for their cries,

The herons would be lost

Amidst the morning snow.

CHIYO-NI

We even stare at horses

On this snowy morning.

BASHŌ

In the spring rain

All things grow beautiful.

CHIYO-NI

The white chrysanthemums at dawn

Look taller than they are.

YASEN

I break my fast

Amidst the morning glory.

BASHŌ

How refreshing

To watch the gates in the morning

As grass is carried in.

BONCHŌ

Like the morning glory

How fleeting is my life

Today ... and then ... ?

MORITAKE

Take me with you

Fly free from servitude

My kite.

TAMA

My gardener of chrysanthemums

You are become their servant.

BUSON

The Witherer blows

And day by day

The wild ducks are more beautiful.

SHIRŌ

The first snow

Just enough to bend the jonquil leaves.

BASHŌ

The black crow that I always despised,

And yet, against the snowy dawn . . .

BASHŌ

If I were the emperor

Of a deserted island

It would be nice.

SŌSEKI

The water birds seem heavy

But they float.

ONITSURA

Like a morning glory

My life itself seems today.

MORITAKE

This morning

The snow turned to rain,

The fault of nearing spring.

SAMPŪ

The pure morning dew

Has no use for this world.

ISSA

As day breaks

All around the castle

The cries of ducks.

KYOROKU

Ah ... the morning glory ...

Even you have let me down.

BASHŌ

A sight to behold on New Year's Day

For this I keep Mount Fuji.

SŌKAN

Without my journey,

And without the spring,

I would have missed this dawn.

SHIKI

DAYLIGHT

清暉

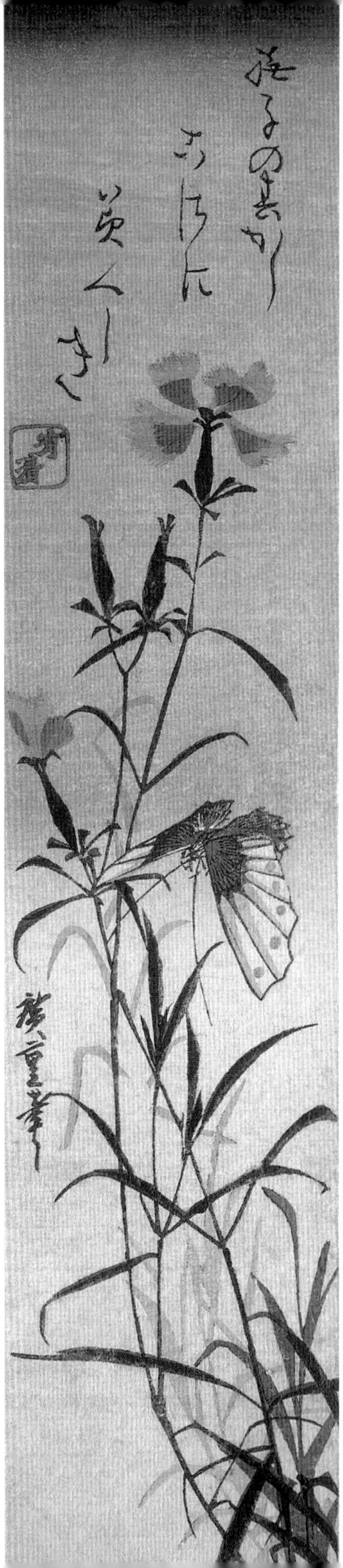

A fallen flower

Flew back to its perch

A butterfly.

MORITAKE

Without a brush

The willow paints the wind.

SARYŪ

Amidst the summer grasses

Lie the graves of Saga's beauties.

SHIKI

At the ancient pond

A frog jumped

With a splash.

BASHŌ

If seen by day

A firefly

Is just a red-necked bug.

BASHŌ

Its sail dips in the sea

The ship on the spring waters.

OTSUJI

When the cherry blossoms bloomed

They brought beauty to my heart.

TATSU-JO

The wild geese

Ate my young blades of barley

But see them go ...

YASUI

清
暉

Clouds come

Clouds go

Above the maple leaves

At the waterfall.

SŌSEKI

Both stones and trees

Glare on the eye

In this heat.

KYORAI

The summer river has a bridge

But horses through the water wade.

SHIKI

Not spring nor autumn

None touch the heights of Fuji.

BAISHITSU

A cloud of flowers

A bell rings

At Ueno? Or Asakusa?

BASHŌ

In the spring breeze

Chewing on his pipe

Waits the venerable ferryman.

BASHŌ

Across the summer stream

With such joy

My sandals in my hand.

BUSON

The summer grasses

As if the warriors were a dream.

BASHŌ

The nightingale

Behind the willow

Before the grove.

BASHŌ

Oh my ... Oh my ...

Was all I could say

Of the flowers on Mount Yoshino.

TEISHITSU

The pedlar

Harassed by a barking dog

Beneath peach trees in bloom.

BUSON

The woodpecker searches for dead trees

Amidst the blossoms.

JŌSŌ

Flowers from an unknown tree

Filled me with their fragrance.

BASHŌ

Oh butterfly

What are you dreaming of

When you move your wings?

CHIYO-NI

Great Buddha

Even while sleeping

Gets flowers and gold.

ISSA

While they are away

Leaves pile up

In the gardens of the gods.

BASHŌ

The scarlet leaves of autumn

Pale before the sight

Of waving green rice fields.

KIKUSHA-NI

The wings of passing birds

Singed on the red maple leaves.

SHIKŌ

DUSK

Oh leaves, ask the wind which of you

Will be the first to fall.

SŌSEKI

All crying done

Nothing remains

But the shell of a cicada.

BASHŌ

Along this road

Is none but I

This autumn eve.

BASHŌ

As dusk dulls the eyes of hawks

Now the quails begin to chirp.

BASHŌ

On the great bell

Stops a butterfly

And sleeps.

BUSON

Today, too

The sun sinks into a world of mustard flowers.

TANTAN

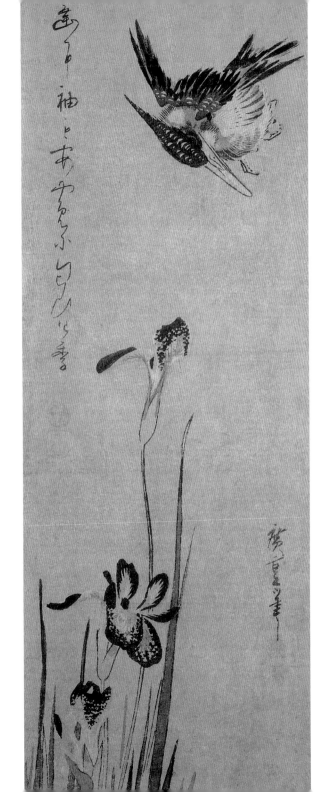

The mountain stream

Milled the rice for me

While I took a nap.

ISSA

With the air of a century past

The fallen leaves on the garden.

BASHŌ

On New Year's Day

I am as lonely

As an autumn eve.

BASHŌ

黄
昏

After a long day

With contagious yawns

We parted.

SŌSEKI

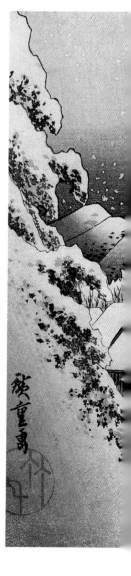

On the old pond

Snow falls on the mandarin ducks

This evening.

SHIKI

Without white hairs

Wither the willow leaves.

SHOKYŪ-NI

大隅
櫻島

Even if the cherry flowers bloom

Ours is a world of suffering.

ISSA

For the man who says

He tires of his child

There are no flowers.

BASHŌ

The burning sun

Sunk in the sea

By the Mogami river.

BASHŌ

My hunter of dragonflies

How far would he have strayed today?

CHIYO-NI

DUSK 61

To land after land without time

The wild geese return.

SHUMPA

Both field and mountain

All taken by the snow

Till nothing yet remains.

JŌSŌ

Since you went away

No flowers are left on earth.

SŌSEKI

The winter gale

Blows the evening sun

Into the sea.

Tired and worn

Seeking an inn

I stopped to gaze at wisteria flowers.

BASHŌ

The evening breeze

Blows ripples 'gainst

The blue heron's legs.

BUSON

黄
昏

That soon they will die

Is unknown

To the chirping cicadas.

BASHŌ

In the blue darkening sky

The moon paints a pine tree.

RANSETSU

Never to be butterflies

Blown by the autumn wind

The sorry mustard worms.

BASHŌ

MOONLIGHT

月光

Through May showers

One night, as if in secret

The moon in the pines.

RYŌTA

In the moonlight

There were flowers

But it was just a field of cotton.

BASHŌ

A cuckoo calls

And through the great bamboo grove

I see the moon.

BASHŌ

The autumn moon

Shining so brightly

So I wrote this.

SEKKEI

Watching the cormorant fishing boats

In time

I was full of sorrow.

BASHŌ

信

Some villages have no sea bream

Some no flowers

But all see tonight's moon.

SAIKAKU

The fireflies

Fear their reflection

In the water.

SUTE-JO

In the octopus's jar

A fleeting dream

Beneath the summer moon.

BASHŌ

月
光

Walking along

My shadow beside me

Watching the moon.

SODŌ

With the passing of the rains

The lava is cool

On Mount Asama.

SODŌ

At the same lodging

Slept some courtesans,

Lespedeza flowers and the moon.

BASHŌ

The sky clears

And the moon and the snow

Are one colour.

SOGETSU-NI

On the darkening sea

The voices of wild ducks

Are faint and white.

BASHŌ

The sea is wild

And all the way to Sado island

The River of Heaven.

BASHŌ

Hang the net

And even the mosquitoes are pretty

Flying through the moonbeams.

BAISHITSU

Watched I the moon without tiring

Not once nor twice.

KIGIN

Do you cry

To drive my mother from my dreams

Cuckoo.

KIKAKU

品川
見越ノ
月

A bank of clouds

Bears the moon upon it.

BONCHŌ

Great is his learning

Who is blind to insight in the lightning.

BASHŌ

With one who does not speak his every thought

I spend a pleasant evening.

HYAKUCHI

It grows late

Reflected in the rice fields

The Milky Way.

IZEN

Cry not, insects

For even stars in love

Must endure separation.

ISSA

The sweet spring night

Of cherry blossom viewing

Has ended.

BASHŌ

月
光

About the Poems

(p.13) Fukuda Chiyo-Ni (1701–75) is often regarded as Japan's greatest female haiku poet. Born in Matsutō (Kaga province), she was married at nineteen, widowed at twenty-seven and lost her only son when she was twenty-eight, which led to her to compose her most famous work 'My Hunter of Dragonflies' (page 60). Here she observes how those who rise early for prayers are alone with nature.

(p.13) A similar work from Chiyo-Ni, which this time uses just sound and the absence of image to paint a picture of white herons.

(p.13) Born Matsuo Jinshichirō, but better known to posterity as Bashō (1644–94), the most famous haiku poet was the son of a low-ranking samurai of Iga province. At the age of nine, he became a page-boy to Yoshitada, ruler of Ueno castle and a poet himself using the pen-name Sengin. Bashō studied poetry under Yoshitada until his master's death when, distraught, he renounced the world to devote himself to poetry and Zen Buddhism. He lived in a hut by a pond, in the shade of a banana tree (*bashō* is Japanese for 'banana tree'). Here Bashō describes how the land is changed so much by snowfall that he and his companions see commonplace things in a new light – even the horses they would normally ignore as they passed on the road.

(p.14) Chiyo-Ni is praising a fresh outlook on life as well as the dewy glow after the rains. She was to write a similar poem in her old age, likening herself to the willow which, though stout, still has grace.

(p.14) Nakamura Yasen (dates unknown) was born in Sagami province and was a disciple of Ryūkyo. In this poem, the poet applies an artist's appreciation of light and perspective through words.

(p.15) In English, as in Japanese, the double meaning of 'morning glory' adds another level to the simple statement. Bashō wrote this poem to chastise his favourite pupil Kikaku, whom he thought was overindulging in food and drink. The flowers of the *Convolvulus* or morning glory appear early but are gone by midday.

(p.15) Nozawa Bonchō (?–1714), also sometimes known as Miyagi Bonchō, was a disciple of Bashō. Born in Kanazawa, he lived for most of his life in Kyōto (the old Japanese capital in Yamashiro province) where he worked as a physician. Here he is either pleased at the sight of fresh fodder or at others doing all the work while he watches.

(p.16) Arakida Moritake (1472–1549) was a high priest at the Great Ise Shrines. In this poem, he uses the morning glory, which flowers at dawn and fades by noon, to represent the fleeting nature of life.

(p.16) Tama (dates unknown) was a courtesan, kept imprisoned in a licensed red-light district. Here she asks to be set free. It is only with the final line that we discover she is talking to a paper kite that can neither hear nor help her – a fact that increases the sense of melancholy. In this translation, the word 'my' has been added for scansion. It is more likely that Tama is merely looking from a window at a kite that is not even hers.

(p.16) Taniguchi Buson (1715–83) was born in a small village near Ōsaka. After a happy childhood cut short by the death of his parents, he became an apprentice to the poet Hajin. An artist as well as a poet, Buson's name literally means 'Turnip Town', though some authorities have suggested this is a frivolous rendering of the true meaning 'Deserted Village'. Buson's point here is that no one can succeed at a pursuit without devoting themselves to it and that devotion to anything is a full-time job.

(p.19) Inoue Shirō (1742–1813) came from Nagoya (Owari province). He was a physician and a disciple of Kyōdai. The *kogarashi* wind or 'Witherer' mentioned in this poem would blow in late autumn. It was a sign that winter was truly on its way.

(p.19) Pressure that barely bends a fragile leaf is hardly pressure at all, but this is the first breath of winter's cold and Bashō sees what is to come.

(p.19) Here Bashō is saying that often it is our perception that changes, rather than the objects we perceive.

(p.20) Natsume Sōseki (1867–1916) was born in Edo (later renamed Tōkyō). He was a famous poet, Anglophile and author of many books, including *Kokoro* and *The Three-Cornered World*. Here he is feeling miserable and would prefer to be alone. The translation deliberately uses the neutral, clichéd 'nice' for the equally-clichéd *suzushi*, normally rendered as 'cool' or 'refreshing'.

(p.23) Kamijima Onitsura (1660–1738) came from Itami (Settsu province) and was a pupil of Sō-in. Here he comments that no matter how unwieldy waterfowl may look on land, they can manage perfectly well in their own element.

(p.23) This is Moritake's *jisei*, or death-bed poem, in which he compares his threescore years and ten to the swift passing of a *Convolvulus* flower.

(p.23) Sugiyama Sampū (1646–1732) was born in Edo and sold fish to the Shōgun and his retainers. Here he sulks about the absence of picturesque snow to write about and finds that, in doing so, he has found another subject.

(p.25) Kobayashi Issa (1763–1827) was a farmer's son from Kashiwabara, which might explain his matter-of-fact style. Here he places the purity of the dew in opposition with the world at large, reminding us that the world is not necessarily there for our benefit, any more than it is there for the dew's.

(p.25) Morikawa Kyoroku (1655–1715) was a samurai in the clan of Hikone. Many of his best poems combine the military and the everyday, such as this juxtaposition of secular politics and the natural world.

(p.25) A surprising verse, again showing that Bashō was not afraid to break the haiku style. Beginning as another tender ode to the short-lived morning glory flower, it suddenly becomes a description of an old man in a bad mood. But there is also humour here, as Bashō swats one of his poetic subjects out of the way. His ability to laugh at himself is part of his genius.

(p.26) Born in Ōmi province and a one-time servant to the Shōgun Ashikaga Yoshihisa, Yamazaki Sōkan (1458–1546) later became a poet and hermit. Here he appears to belittle Mount Fuji though he is really saying that it is too beautiful to gaze upon every day and should be saved for special occasions.

(p.26) Masaoka Shiki (1856–1902) was born in Iyo province and was a samurai from the Matsuyama clan. He says nothing of the dawn itself but merely lists the factors that have combined to make it so wonderful. There is an element of melancholy – how many other dawns has he missed?

(p.31) Mistaking a butterfly for a flower, Moritake is reminded that nothing is as it seems. A few seconds of the flitting motion of an insect are beautifully encapsulated in the poem. The blossom may die but the butterfly, a symbol of rebirth, points to the cycle of the seasons, in this case the passing from spring to summer.

(p.31) Saryū (surname and dates unknown). Here Saryū describes the wind, which cannot be seen, by its action on the trees – literally the sight of the wind in the willows.

(p.31) This poem is Shiki's variation on Bashō's verse, 'The summer grasses', composed at Takadachi fort in the far north of Japan (page 40). Here he comments on the long-gone women of Saga (outside Kyōto) whose beauty may once have been great but is now turned to dust.

(p.32) This is arguably Bashō's most famous poem. The poet was himself to claim that it encapsulated every element of his style, and that every verse he composed afterwards was merely a variation on the theme. It mixes a deep sense of tradition (the ancient pond) with the heedless natural world (the frog) and an iconoclastic splash – an instant preserved forever in poetry.

(p.33) Bashō reminds us that we are surrounded by illusion and different environments can give different perspectives on the same thing. The beautiful night-time firefly is made commonplace by the light of day.

(p.35) Ōsuga Otsuji (1881–1919) was born in Fukushima province. He was a teacher of Japanese literature. Here he evokes the idea of rough seas simply by noting that the ship's sails dip as low as the water.

(p.35) Little is known about Tatsu-Jo, a female poet alive during the nineteenth century. In this poem, a woman, unsure of herself, gains confidence when she sees the cherry blossoms.

(p.35) Okada Yasui (1657–1743) was a merchant from Nagoya (Owari province) who became a pupil of Bashō. This haiku perfectly captures the contradiction of businessman and poet within Yasui, as he rails at the birds for eating his crops while quietly marvelling at the sight of them in flight.

(p.37) Sōseki's poem is circular. Is it a camera-shot that pans down from the clouds in the sky to the trees and the water? Or does it start with autumn leaves in the water, which also reflects the clouds?

(p.37) Mukai Kyorai (1651–1704) was a disciple of Bashō. Born to a Confucianist father in Nagasaki (Hizen province), he lived in Kyōto. The poem sums up the unbearable temperature of summer, when light and heat combine to make the simplest action uncomfortable. Here stones and trees, innocuous subjects of countless poems, force the poet to avert his eyes.

(p.37) When the river falls to a trickle, the bridge is part of the view but not necessary for daily life. But the river will one day swell again; this new path across is temporary, like life itself.

(p.39) Sakurai Baishitsu (1768–1852) came from Kanazawa (Kaga province) and became a retainer of the Kaga clan, where he was a 'connoisseur of swords' (a collector of swords). Upon retirement, he became a poet in Kyōto. Here he notes that, although poets have praised it in all seasons, the peak of Mount Fuji is always in winter.

(p.39) One of Bashō's most famous poems, inspired by the view through the summer haze of cherry blossom on both sides of the Sumida river.

(p.39) Bashō juxtaposes the honorific -dono, used for lords and great knights, with the image of a boatman smoking his pipe and waiting for customers. The boatman may be a commoner but he is master of his vessel.

(p.40) Even in joy there is sadness. This happy vision of paddling in a brook is a glimpse of an instant several centuries old.

(p.40) Bashō composed this verse at the ruins of Takadachi fort, where the hero Yoshitsune and his last loyal retainers made a brave but futile stand against overwhelming odds in 1189. Hundreds of years later, it is hard to believe that such a peaceful site witnessed those events. In the original Japanese, the final phrase *yume no ato* ('after a dream') has a double meaning – that

Yoshitsune's noble ideals died with him. Years later, the poet Shiki would compose a similar verse in imitation (page 31).

(p.40) The *uguisu* or Japanese nightingale is larger than the European version and sings during the day. But, as with many other birds, they can be difficult to locate and even during the daylight are often known only by their song.

(p.42) Yasubara Teishitsu (1609–73) came from Kyōto. He was a pupil of the poet Teitoku. The poet is rendered mute by the sight of the cherry blossoms on Mount Yoshino in Yamato province. This is a Zen moment that silences the master of haiku. The poem shows considerable humility and allows the image to speak for itself. Although this is a well-known verse in Japan, some critics have pointed out that it says very little and could be applied to virtually anything. Said once it is a moving verse; said twice it is a cliché.

(p.42) Buson reminds us that we can find beauty in everything, even when we are occupied with the concerns of the world.

(p.42) A variant on our own 'unable to see the wood for the trees'; here the bird is going about its business, oblivious to the beauty around it.

(p.44) Bashō composed this verse at the Great Ise Shrines, the most sacred in Japan. Beyond the material environment, he detected something unnameable, indescribable: he was in the presence of divinity.

(p.44) A butterfly will sometimes perch very still on a flower, its listless wings flapping only occasionally. Chiyo-Ni wonders if the butterfly is asleep and of what it might be dreaming. Her poem recalls the words of the Chinese philosopher Zhuang Zi, who asked himself whether he was a man dreaming he was a butterfly, or a butterfly dreaming he was a man.

(p.44) In this humorous verse, Issa reminds us that the truly enlightened have given up striving in the material world. And that the most enlightened of them, the Buddha himself, receives donations without any effort at all.

(p.47) According to Japanese tradition, October is the 'godless month', when all the spirits in Japan attend a conference at the Great Idzumo Shrine. This humorous poem describes Bashō's visit to the Gongen Shrine in Numazu (Suruga province) during this month, when the neglected state of the garden did indeed suggest that the boss was away on business.

(p.47) Tagami Kikusha-Ni (1752–1826) came from Chōfu (Nagato province). She became a pupil of Sankyō and made a pilgrimage through Japan. Here she breaks with tradition by asserting that spring is more beautiful than autumn, and that the arrival of new life is a better subject for poetry than autumnal decline.

(p.47) Kagami Shikō (1664–1731) was born in Kitano (Mino province) and was first a Buddhist priest, then a physician. In the original of this poem, the use of the word *momiji* (the Japanese for 'maple' and 'autumn leaves'; literally 'red leaves') together with a verb associated with burning evokes the bright red of fire, without Shikō having to use the word itself.

(p.51) Sōseki wrote this poem from his sickbed when he thought he was dying. In the Japanese poetic tradition, ageing men are often likened to autumn leaves.

(p.51) This poem is not well regarded by critics, but contains the beautifully tragic idea that the *semi*, or Japanese cicada, cries itself to death.

(p.51) In September 1694, Bashō was approaching a tea house in Ōsaka (Settsu province) when he realized that he was the only one on the road. With hindsight, the poem gains extra poignance since Bashō did not have long to live.

(p.52) The subject of the poem is just a noise in the twilight; but it takes a poet's sensibility to notice its origin. Unable to hunt in the twilight, birds of prey are no longer a threat.

(p.52) Some translators have added the phrase 'Until it rings', but this statement of the obvious breaks the mood of the haiku.

(p.52) Matsuki Tantan (1675–1761) was born in Ōsaka and became a pupil of Kikaku. Just north of Osaka is Biwa, Japan's largest lake, which has long been surrounded by field after field of waving mustard seed. Here Tantan watches the sunset but also considers that every day can be as beautiful as this – one just needs to know where to look.

(p.55) A dozing miller in particular might see eternity and contentment in a water-mill; not because it is turned by the icy waters of a mountain stream but because it makes his life easier.

(p.55) While visiting his pupil Riyū at the Myōshōji temple at Hirata (Ōmi province), Bashō took time to admire the garden, full of moss and ancient trees, which has genuinely been nurtured for over a hundred years.

(p.55) Amid the celebrations and joy of the New Year, Bashō reminds us that it is still possible to be lonely in a crowd.

(p.56) Sōseki was in Matsuyama where he met his friend Kyoshi. His poem on their parting sums up a long spring day of catching up on old times.

(p.56) In this poem, Shiki both expands and contracts the focus of the initial image, zooming in to show the detail of snow and ducks, then out to show the night sky.

(p.56) Yagu Fumi, otherwise known as Shokyū-Ni (1713–81), came from Chikuzen province where she was secretary to the poet Yaha. Here, after the death of her husband, she laments the fact that human ageing is not as pretty as the colourful death of leaves.

(p.59) Issa finds beauty and sadness hand-in-hand and urges us to accept that life is what we make it.

(p.59) A humbling poem that seeks to remind Bashō's pupils that the appreciation of nature should not come at the expense of one's responsibilities.

(p.59) This poem uses an unexpected choice of words to give a new perspective on an ordinary sunset. Bashō has deliberately used *sunk* instead of *sank*, *by* instead of *near*, in order to imply that the setting sun has been washed into the ocean by the river itself.

(p.60) In this, her most famous poem, Chiyo-Ni writes of a devastating loss. Her son's death means she need never worry about him or chide him again.

(p.63) Shimomura Shumpa (1749–1810) was a merchant in Kyōto and a pupil of the master Kito. His descendants would found the Daimaru drapers company (now a huge multinational corporation). In this poem, he speculates on the geese who follow the winter, flying from country to country, seemingly without any sense of calendar (here translated as 'time'). Does this mean that the geese live beyond time, in a world where it is always winter? 'Without' is used here in its arcane English sense of 'beyond' or 'outside'.

(p.63) Naitō Jōsō (1661–1704) was a samurai in the clan of Inuyama in Owari province. Later he became a Buddhist priest. This poem, usually given the title 'Silver World', depicts a paragon of nothingness. It reflects on the Zen idea of space saying more than the lines; the Japanese equivalent of a white dove in a snowstorm. How can one illustrate the unseeable, except with a picture of nothing?

(p.63) The subject of the poem is a lover of Sōseki, a beautiful woman who died young.

(p.64) Compare Sōseki's poem to its antecedent by Bashō (page 59).

(p.64) Bashō was entering the town of Tambaichi (Yamato province) when he saw the blooms and forgot his long day.

(p.64) Here Buson uses the haiku motif of 'refreshment', juxtaposing the cool slosh of the ripples with the colour blue, itself evocative of coolness and relaxation.

(p.66) Buddhism teaches that life is but a 'bridge of dreams', a tiny moment of insight in an infinity of darkness. In this poem, Bashō artfully dwells on the short-lived insects, using the silence after the poem to turn the focus of attention onto the listener.

(p.66) Hattori Ransetsu (1653–1707) came from Enami (Awaji province), where he was a low-ranking samurai. He later became a Buddhist priest. The eerie image in this poem – the silhouette of a pine tree actually painted on the sky – is very rare in haiku.

(p.66) The mustard worm never turns into a butterfly but dies with the onset of autumn – a sobering metaphor for mankind.

(p.71) Ōshima Ryōta (1707–87) lived in Edo (Kai Province) and was a pupil of Ritō. This famous poem has been discredited by some critics for attributing a personality to the moon but, as a close reading shows, this is not so.

(p.71) Humble cotton is transformed into a carpet of white flowers in the moonlight. In mistaking cotton for flowers, the poet displays his own romantic heart.

(p.71) Bashō wrote this in the village of Saga (outside Kyōto) which is full of bamboo groves. Japanese tradition holds that bamboo groves are haunted. The Japanese cuckoo has a shrill cry – perhaps Bashō is scaring himself.

(p.72) Sekkei (dates and surname unknown). His blunt ode to the moon is perhaps the best example of haiku stripped bare. There is nothing to the poem at all – to understand Sekkei, you will have to look at the moon yourself. If you can look at the moon, no poem can compare.

(p.72) Bashō was watching the fishing boats on the Nagara River (Mino province) where each fisherman employs a dozen trained cormorants on lines. By the bright light of torches, the birds dive below the surface and when they catch a fish are dragged back to the boat. Unable to swallow their prey because of a whalebone ring about their throats, the cormorants are forced to regurgitate their hard-won trout – a sight which moved the poet to sadness.

(p.75) Ihara Saikaku (1641–93) was a pupil of Sō-in but is better known as a novelist. His works include *The Life of an Amorous Man* and *Five Women Who Loved Love*. Here he reminds us that, no matter how far apart two places may be, they all see the same moon.

(p.75) Den Sute-Jo (1633–98) became a Buddhist nun following the death of her magistrate husband. She was a pupil of Kigin. The poem has a light tone but perhaps the fireflies are right to be afraid – if they get too close to their reflections they will drown.

(p.75) While on a ship off Akashi Bay (on Japan's inland sea), Bashō thought he saw an octopus stirring listlessly in one of the fishermen's traps, unaware that its reverie would soon be over, along with its life. But, as always, there is another reading. The 'fleeting dream' is life itself, and the simple octopus is no different from the poet who watches it.

(p.76) Yamaguchi Sodō (1641–1716) came to Edo, where he became a pupil of Kigin. The original Japanese is more properly 'my shadow seeing me home', as if the shadow is leading the way and the poet only following. This clever reversal shows the constantly questioning nature of haiku. Humans cannot possess their shadows and even the moon has no light of its own. All things are shadows, as all things are dreams.

(p.76) A poem that captures the idea of oppressive summer heat wiped away by a sudden storm. Mount Asama, near Karuizawa (Shinano province), is the largest active volcano in Japan.

(p.76) In the village of Ichifuri (Echigo province), Bashō found himself staying at the same inn as two prostitutes. True to form, Bashō watched the moon and garden flowers through the night. When next day the ladies asked him to accompany them to Ise, he declined with this flustered poem.

(p.79) Sogetsu-Ni (?–1804) came from Miharu (Iwashiro province). She was the wife of another poet, Tsunemaru. Her poem about the moon and snow, misleadingly simple, raises questions in the mind of the reader. Is the snow so bright that it is as bright as the moon? Or is the moon so bright that it matches the snow? Words are clearly not enough.

(p.79) Bashō supposedly wrote this poem one night at Owari (off the coast of modern-day Nagoya), when the only two appreciable features in the dark were the white tops of distant breakers and the calls of unseen ducks.

(p.79) Bashō composed this verse at the port of Izumozaki (in Echigo province) where, on a clear night, he could see the distant island of Sado some sixty miles away. Above the high seas glimmers the Milky Way (the 'River of Heaven').

(p.80) Sakurai Baishitsu (1768–1852) began life as a connoisseur of swords before becoming a poet in Kyōto. Here Baishitsu shows that, to a poet, even mosquitoes can be beautiful – all that is required is a net to remove their physical annoyance.

(p.80) Kitamura Kigin (1623–1705) was a Shinto priest from Ōmi province. Here he juxtaposes the need for sleep with the beauty of the moon, and tells that he could not tear his eyes away, no matter how late it became.

(p.80) Takarai Kikaku (1660–1707) was a physician's son, and Bashō's favourite disciple (see note to page 15). His mother died when he was a young man and this poem was composed to the bird whose calling woke him from a nightmare.

(p.83) Bonchō's eye for coincidences (such as the way the moon might appear to rest on the clouds) is one of the traits that mark him out as a favourite of modern critics.

(p.83) Bashō was annoyed with those poets and philosophers who thought there was nothing more to haiku than an observation followed by a comment on the transience of existence. This poem was written to commemorate a Buddhist sage who commented that 'A little knowledge of Zen is a dangerous thing'. Bashō agreed wholeheartedly, and wrote this haiku in deliberate contradiction of his normal style. For this reason it is often ignored by critics, who do not want to consider that Bashō might have tired of his imitators.

(p.83) Teramura Hyakuchi (1748–1836) was a merchant's son from Kyōto who became a pupil of Buson. Here he reminds us that when there is nothing to say it is better to say nothing.

(p.84) Hirose Izen (?–1710) was a pupil of Bashō from Minō province. The profound calm required to reflect dim stars in water adds to the late-night feel of Izen's poem.

(p.84) This poem refers to the Chinese myth of the lovelorn Weaver and Herder Stars, who can only cross the River of Heaven (the Milky Way) once a year, on 7 July. When even stars must be apart, the cries of insects (and human beings) seem all the more insignificant.

(p.84) The poem tells of the end of an evening but, seeing nothing of beauty there, Bashō returns to the highlight of the night – the cherry blossom viewing – noting only how quickly time has passed.

Afterword

This book combines paintings and woodblock prints (mainly of the Edo Period, 1603–1867), from the renowned collection at The Art Institute of Chicago, with haiku by leading Japanese poets of the fifteenth century onward. It was during the Edo Period that this mode of poetry assumed the independent form by which we know it today, was given the name 'haiku', and enjoyed great popularity. Thus it is not surprising that the painters and graphic artists of the Edo era often used ellipsis, suggestive but unexpected juxtapositions, and deceptive simplicity – all elements of haiku – to engage the imagination of the viewer in a similar way as poets used these techniques to involve the reader. In fact, a number of Edo Period painters were poets and vice versa.

In Japan, poetry and painting have always been considered sister arts. Poets and painters kept company, collaborated on a variety of artistic projects (including books), and engaged in one another's disciplines – not as an amusing pastime but as a serious artistic endeavour. Japanese poets and painters traditionally have displayed great sensitivity to the changing beauty and particularity of the seasons. The poet could never forgo communion with the living world; obliviousness to the seasons was seen as dissonant and even diseased. Similarly, indications of the seasons – such as a flower, a bird or specific human activity – were essential components of the painter's vocabulary.

Before the seventeenth century, poems were written to a metre of thirty-one syllables, in groupings of 5-7-5 and 7-7. It was the Zen Buddhist monk Matsuo Bashō (1644–94) who took the form to new heights, expressing strength, humanity and religious understanding within an even more austere format – the 5-7-5 syllable haiku. Inspired primarily by the remote landscapes through which he travelled, he intended his poetry to capture the spirit of the high tradition of monochrome ink painting. Rarely coloured and giving only indications of the whole, this style of painting (an example is featured on the endpapers of this book) invokes an awareness of the present that permits access to higher truths. As Bashō put it, he wanted to convey the sense of 'unchanging amid the flow' – a very Zen expression of the shifting materiality of the instant.

When traditional poets and painters began to work, they embraced the charm and spirit of beauty, the preciousness of a single moment, and the fragrance of multiple meanings. Employing, in the case of the poets, a limited vocabulary of about two thousand words and, in the case of the painters, an established visual language of motifs and brush strokes, these artists presented their audience with the rich associations of their poems and images. Take the line of poetry that is the title of this book: *The Moon in the Pines*. The evergreen pine is called *matsu* in Japan. It grows, carefully groomed, at the entrance to a home; becomes gnarled as it clings to a windswept outlook over the ocean; or serves as an eagle's perch in a high mountain waste. But *matsu* also means 'I'll wait for you' – a very personal promise that never fails to move the hearts of the Japanese toward the evergreen tree. And for both poet and painter, the pine tree is the source of ink. The blackness of the ink, derived from grinding a stick made of the soot of pine charcoal and taken up by the soft tip of a brush, is used to bind words and images to paper.

In its avoidance of the superfluous, in its distilling of an instant, the visual art included here is inspired by the Zen experience – immortalized by Bashō and his followers – of nature and the power of the moment to effect spiritual transformation. Through the ages and to the present day in Japan, the life-giving quality of an ancient poem has been tapped by visiting the spot that witnessed its creation – or simply by reciting it. The poems and images here have been selected to complement one another. Where the translator's words can some-times only approximate the jewel-like facets of the original Japanese idiom, the images may help the reader to access the suspension of time, the 'unchanging amid the flow' that lies at the heart of the poems. I am confident that the juxtaposition of poems and images in this book will suggest layered meanings that neither genre alone can express.

Bernd Jesse, Assistant Curator of Japanese Art

The Art Institute of Chicago

Index of Illustrations

(p.45) Utagawa Hiroshige (1797–1858), *The Drooping Cherries of Yoshino at Ishiyakushi* (*Ishiyakushi Yoshino no Tarezakura*), from the series 'Pastiches from the Pacific Highway' (*Tōkaidō Harimaze Zue*)
Woodblock print
Japan, Edo period, 1836
Frederick W. Gookin Collection, 1939.1205
H. 12.4, W. 13.3

(p.46) Utagawa Kunisada (1786–1864),
Viewing Maple Foliage (*Momijigari no Zu*)
Large (*ōban*) woodblock print
Japan, Edo period, *c.* 1835
Clarence Buckingham Collection, 1925.332
H. 25.5, W. 37.5

(pp.48–9) Utagawa Hiroshige (1797–1858), *Shimmachi Station* (*Shimmachi*), from the series 'The Sixty-nine Stations on the Kiso Road' (*'Kisokaidō Rokujūkyūtsugi no uchi'*)
Detail from large (*ōban*) woodblock print
Japan, Edo period, *c.* 1834–42
Clarence Buckingham Collection, 1925.3721
H. 24.4, W. 36.6

(p.50) Utagawa Hiroshige (1797–1858), *Maple Leaves of Shimosa* (*Shimosa Mama no Momiji*), from the series 'Pastiches with Pictures from all over the Country' (*'Kuni Zukushi Harimaze Zue'*)
Woodblock print
Japan, Edo period, 1852
Clarence Buckingham Collection, 1938.546
H. 21.0, W. 10.8

(p.53) Utagawa Hiroshige (1797–1858), *Kingfisher and Iris*
Detail from half-size poetry-slip (*chūtanzakuban*) woodblock print
Japan, Edo period, *c.* 1835
Clarence Buckingham Collection, 1925.3628
H. 37.5, W. 12.9

(p.54) Kanō Tsunenobu (1636–1713), *Landscape with Waterfall*
Detail from *Summer*, one of three hanging scrolls (*kakejiku*), ink and light colours on silk
Japan, Edo period, late 17th–early 18th century
Samuel Nickerson Endowment Fund, 1933.1653
H. 93.9, W. 32.4

(pp.56–7) Utagawa Hiroshige (1797–1858), *Night Snow at Kambara* (*Kambara Yoru no Yuki*), from the series 'Fifty-three Stations on the Tōkaidō' (*'Tōkaidō Gojūsantsugi no uchi'*)
Detail from large (*ōban*) woodblock print
Japan, Edo period, *c.* 1833
Clarence Buckingham Collection, 1925.3517
H. 24.1, W. 36.8

(p.58) Utagawa Hiroshige (1797–1858), *Sakurajima in Ōsumi* (*Ōsumi Sakurajima*), from the series 'Pastiches with Pictures from all over the Country' (*'Kuni Zukushi Harimaze Zue'*)
Woodblock print
Japan, Edo period, 1852
Frederick W. Gookin Collection, 1939.1227
H. 10.0, W. 12.4

(pp.60–1) Sesshû (1420–1506), *Landscape of the Four Seasons*
Detail from the left side of a pair of six-fold screens, ink and light colours on paper
Japan, Muromachi period, late 15th century
Clarence Buckingham Collection, 1958.403
H. 167.6, W. 358.1

(p.62) Kanō Tsunenobu (1636–1713), *Snowy Landscape*
Detail from *Winter*, one of three hanging scrolls (*kakejiku*), ink and light colours on silk
Japan, Edo period, late 17th–early 18th century

Samuel Nickerson Endowment Fund, 1933.1651
H. 93.9, W. 32.4

(p.65) Utagawa Hiroshige (1797–1858), *The Shore at Yokka'ichi* (*Yokka'ichi Nakonoura Shinkirō*), from the series 'Pastiches from the Pacific Highway' (*Tōkaidō Harimaze Zue*)
Woodblock print
Japan, Edo period, 1852
Frederick W. Gookin Collection, 1939.1220
H. 16.4, W. 11.2

(p.67) Unkoku Tōeki (1591–1644), *Landscapes*
Left side of a pair of hanging scrolls (*kakejiku*), ink on paper
Japan, Edo period, early 17th century
Clarence Buckingham Collection, 1959.579
H. 97.5, W. 46.3

(pp.68–9) Utagawa Hiroshige (1797–1858), *Autumn Full Moon over the Tama River* (*Tamagawa Shūgetsu*), from the series 'Eight Views from the Environs of Edo' (*'Edo Kinkō Hakkei'*)
Detail from large (*ōban*) woodblock print
Japan, Edo period, *c.* 1838
Clarence Buckingham Collection, 1925.3424
H. 22.8, W. 35.0

(p.70) Utagawa Hiroshige (1797–1858), *Owl on Pine Tree*
Half-size poetry-slip (*chūtanzakuban*) woodblock print
Japan, Edo period, *c.* 1840
Clarence Buckingham Collection, 1925.3625
H. 37.0, W. 13.2

(p.73) Suzuki Harunobu (*c.* 1725–70), *Fidelity* (*Shin*), from a 'Five Cardinal Virtues' series
Detail from half-size (*chūban*) woodblock print
Japan, Edo period, *c.* 1767
Clarence Buckingham Collection, 1928.925
H. 27.2, W. 20.6

(p.74) Katsushika Taito II (1810–53), *Monkey Bridge*
Woodblock print
Japan, Edo period, *c.* 1833
Gift of Chester W. Wright, 1961.173
H. 35.2, W. 24.5

(p.77) Katsushika Hokusai (1760–1849), *The Gatherer of Rushes* (*Tokusakari*), from the series 'The True Mirror of Chinese and Japanese Poetry' (*'Shiika Shashinkyō'*)
Detail from long (*nagaban*) woodblock print
Japan, Edo period, *c.* 1833
Nickerson Collection, 1900.674
H. 50.5, W. 23.1

(p.78) Utagawa Hiroshige (1797–1858), *Snow on the Sumida River* (*Sumida*), from a 'Snow, Moon, and Flowers' set
Large (*ōban*) woodblock print
Japan, Edo period, *c.* 1836
Gift of Gaylord Donnelley, 1969.693
H. 24.9, W. 37.3

(p.81) Kobayashi Kiyochika (1847–1915), *Moonlight Evening at Shinagawa* (*Shinagawa Mikoshi no Tsuki*), from the series 'One Hundred Views of Musashi Province' (*'Musashi Hyakkei no uchi'*)
Detail from large (*ōban*) woodblock print
Japan, Edo period, *c.* 1879
Clarence Buckingham Collection, 1936.232
H. 32.5, W. 21.5

(p.85) Ogata Gekkō (1859–1920), *Full Moon and Autumn Flowers*
Fan paper (*uchiwa-e*) woodblock print
Japan, Meiji period, *c.* 1895
Gift of Allan Mitchell, 1976.553
H. 24.7, W. 24.6